TRIALS BIKES

BY **THOMAS STREISSGUTH**

BELLWETHER MEDIA · MINNEAPOLIS, MN

™

Are you ready to take it to the extreme?
Torque books thrust you into the action-packed
world of sports, vehicles, and adventure. These books
may include dirt, smoke, fire, and dangerous stunts.
WARNING: Read at your own risk.

Library of Congress Cataloging-in-Publication Data

Streissguth, Thomas, 1958–
  Trials bikes / by Thomas Streissguth.
     p. cm. – (Torque–motorcycles)
  Summary: "Full color photography accompanies engaging information about Trials Bikes,
The combination of high-interest subject matter and light text is intended for students in
grades 3 through 7"–Provided by publisher.
  Includes bibliographical references and index.
  ISBN-13: 978–1–60014–160–7 (hardcover : alk. paper)
  ISBN-10: 1–60014–160–9 (hardcover : alk. paper)
  1. Trials bikes (Motorcycles)–Juvenile literature. 2. Motorcycling–Competitions–Juvenile
literature. I. Title.

  TL441.S77 2008
  629.227'5–dc22   2007040750

This edition first published in 2008 by Bellwether Media.

CONTENTS

WHAT IS A TRIALS BIKE?

A trials bike is a special kind of off-road motorcycle. Trials bikes are used for riding through big obstacle courses.

A trials bike has little or
no seat. The rider almost
always stands up while
riding. Riders try not to
touch the ground with any
part of their body. They use
their bodies to keep perfect
control of the bike.

Trials bike riders move steadily down steep, muddy paths on their motorcycles.

Taking sharp curves and jumping huge boulders are thrilling parts of trials bike riding. It's not racing. It is a test of a rider's skill and strength over the **terrain**.

FEATURES

Trials bikes are not built for speed. They are built for tricky maneuvers. Top speed on a trials course is only about 50 miles (80 kilometers) per hour. The lightweight aluminum frame of a trials bike allows the rider to easily handle the bike at low speeds. The frame has about one foot of **clearance** to get over obstacles.

Trials bike tires are specialized for rough ground. The tires are made of soft rubber. The air pressure in the tires is low. The soft rubber and low air pressure help the tires grip dirt and mud.

Trials bike engines must be powerful in order to handle the challenging maneuvers of the course. Engines are measured in cubic centimeters (cc). Trials bikes have engine sizes ranging from 125cc to 1000cc. They are water-cooled. Water carries heat away from the engine much faster than air can. Water-cooling allows higher **horsepower** without increasing the size of the engine. The engines can give plenty of power to handle steep slopes. The **gearbox** has five speeds.

Riders must use safety equipment. Taking a spill on rough ground can cause a bad injury. Helmets and gloves are essential to a rider's safety. Expert riders always wear protective clothing.

FAST FACT

TRIALS BIKES ARE MADE BY GAS GAS, MONTESA, HONDA, AND BETA.

TRIALS BIKES
IN ACTION

Trials bike competitions are full of challenges. The courses are always over rough terrain such as hills, mountains, and deserts. Riders go through the course one at a time. **Observers** watch the riders closely throughout the course. They count the number of times the rider touches the ground. Touching the ground is called a **dab**.

FAST FACT

TRIALS RIDERS COMPETE IN CLASSES DIVIDED BY SKILL LEVEL. THE SIX CLASSES OF OBSERVED TRIALS COMPETITION ARE NOVICE, SPORTSMAN, INTERMEDIATE, ADVANCED, MASTER, AND EXPERT.

A perfect run is called a **"clean"** and gets a score of 0. A score of 5 is the worst possible score in trials competitions. It is called a **"fiasco."** It means you didn't finish, stalled out, fell, went backwards, or dabbed the ground too many times. The rider with the lowest overall score after several runs earns the trophy.

Competitive trials riding demands balance, concentration, strength, and lots of practice. It tests the body and mind of the rider. Riders get a few practice runs before every event. They have to memorize the terrain. They have to plan their run carefully. In the course of a run, a top rider performs tricks such as **air turns**, **bunny hops**, and **wheelies**. Trials riding is a challenging test of motorcycle handling skills.

FAST FACT

TRIALS BIKE RIDING IS ESPECIALLY BIG IN AUSTRALIA AND EUROPE. MANY OF THE RECENT WORLD CHAMPIONS ARE FROM SPAIN AND BRITAIN. THE AMAZING DOUGIE LAMPKIN, A BRITISH RIDER, WON SEVEN WORLD CHAMPIONSHIPS IN A ROW.

GLOSSARY

air turn–a trick that involves turning a trials bike in mid-air

bunny hop–a jump on a motorcycle done by a rider without the use of a ramp

clean–the completion of a trials bike course without any body part touching the ground

clearance–the distance between the frame of a vehicle and the ground

dab–when a rider touches the ground during a run

fiasco–a score of 5, the worst possible score on a trials course

gearbox–the engine part that controls a trials bike's gears

horsepower–the measure of an engine's power

observer–an official who watches a trials bike rider to keep score

terrain–the natural surface features of the land

wheelie–a bike maneuver in which the motorcycle is ridden on the back tire only

TO LEARN MORE

AT THE LIBRARY

Armentrout, David and Patricia. *Dirt Bikes*. Vero Beach, Fla.: Rourke, 2006.

David, Jack. *Motocross Racing*. Minneapolis, Minn.: Bellwether, 2008.

Levy, Janey. *Motocross Races*. New York: PowerKids Press, 2007.

Parr, Danny. *Dirt Bikes*. Minneapolis, Minn.: Capstone, 2002.

ON THE WEB

Learning more about motorcycles is as easy as 1, 2, 3.

1. Go to www.factsurfer.com

2. Enter "motorcycles" into search box.

3. Click the "Surf" button and you will see a list of related web sites.

With factsurfer.com, finding more information is just a click away.

INDEX

The images in this book are reproduced through the courtesy of: Vic Pigula/Alamy, front cover, p. 13; Joe Hawkins Photography/Alamy, pp. 5, 8, 9, 12, 13, 17, 18, 19; imagebroker/Alamy, p. 6; Paolo Stefi, pp. 10, 20; Casey K. Bishop, pp. 14-15.